WHAT PASSES FOR WISDOM

poems by

Bill Ayres

Finishing Line Press
Georgetown, Kentucky

WHAT PASSES FOR WISDOM

ACKNOWLEDGMENTS

"A Bird in the Hand" was published in *Hoot*.
"Two Blessing" was published in *The Anglican Theological Review*.
"Good Morning" was published in *Barely South*.
"Victuals and Speech" was published in *Glass Mountain*.
"I Am the Man Who Yells at His Wife" is in the anthology *What Sort of
      Fuckery is This?*
"Lowered Voices" was in *Plainsongs*.
"The Astronaut's Body" and "The Face of the Clock" were in *Commonweal*.
"Herringbone" was published in *The Roanoke Review*.
"Saint Pops" was in *Inlet*.

Publisher: Leah Maines

Editor: Christen Kincaid

Cover Art: *Snowy Owl,* John James Audubon

Author Photo: Gayle Ayres

Cover Design: Elizabeth Maines McCleavy

Order online: www.finishinglinepress.com
            also available on amazon.com

Author inquiries and mail orders:
Finishing Line Press
P. O. Box 1626
Georgetown, Kentucky 40324
U. S. A.

Table of Contents

PROVERBS

BIBLE STORIES

THIS LIFE

FINALES

1.Proverbs

REBUKE

Three times you tried to catch me.

You grabbed
 as I slipped through your fingers.

You swiped at the blur of blade and handle
as I twisted and spun,

and, then, quickly,
you stooped, stretching,
and reached
as I dropped
point first toward the floor.

Too late, and too late, and too late.

As you bent down to retrieve me,
I thought, "Fool,

could I have been snatched from the air
without squeezing?"

When I want to fall,
let me fall.

I HAVE WORKED FOR A FOOL LONG ENOUGH

One man's trash is another man's treasure

Apple cores, wilted lettuce,
you toss in the garbage under the sink.
I fish them out and take them home.
They make the soil in my garden rich.

The DVD player that broke,
you dropped it in the bin out back.
A little work with a screwdriver
and I got it working again,
found a buyer, fattened my wallet.

Suits too big for you
now that you have lost the weight,
you made a ceremony of burning
in the fire pit on your patio.
I could have tailored them for interview clothes
and found a better paying job.

The rug you tired of,
you had me roll it up and leave it by the curb.

Now my work is done.
I pull my truck around
on my way out.
It doesn't bother me
you read somewhere the color ivory is out of fashion.

Watch as the wife you mocked as pale and weak
helps me pick up the rug
and slide it on the flatbed.
Notice her strong, gold limbs
as she climbs up front.

May the slamming of our cab doors
echo up and down your street
hours after we drive away.

STEED

Displayed, as is proper, in the center of the room
is the horse of the proverbs.
For some reason, a lot of folks
expect her to be white, but, no....

She is housed in the glass case for a reason:
though this mare has been dead many years
some people feel compelled to beat her.

See how skinny she is
—two men were responsible for her feedings.

Observe how the front left hoof is cocked,
revealing that a shoe was lost.

It is a good horse that never stumbles.
This was a very good horse, but
—the point is everyone makes mistakes.

What was that, sir?
No, the reason you don't look a gift horse in the mouth
isn't because she might bite you.
The proverb means—

What? No, it's a blind horse
that can't tell a wink from a nod.
A deaf horse.... Never mind.

And, no, there was nothing wrong
with the horse's back.
The straw you are referring to
was a problem for the camel.

Moving on—that in the corner?
A locked stable door.

LOOKING FOR A NEEDLE...

You notice pretty quickly
some are gold and some are silver,
some are thin and some are thick.
Since it's not you who'll do the sewing,
you never thought to ask what kind of needle.

It's not important now.
You are feeling with your hands more than looking,
steeling yourself for the stinging finger
that will tell you at last you have found it.
One prick and you'll pull your arm up
with a needle stuck in the ball of your thumb
or in the palm of your hand.

At the same time, you are loading the camel,
slinging what you have checked through up onto her hump,
insensitive to how her knees tremble
under her burden of hay.

You don't face her, so you do not see
the hurt in her eyes, in her flanks.
You don't really believe
one more of these straws will snap her spine,
tumbling what you've stacked high down into the street.

If the camel could speak, she would say,
"Rich man, I can carry us both
through the eye of the needle
but not with this load on my back."

TWO CAN KEEP A SECRET IF
ONE OF THEM IS DEAD

Because King Midas liked the country tunes
 more than the classical music of the powers that be
his ears were changed to long and floppy donkey ears.
Midas grew his hair out and pinned them up
under a cowboy hat.
The thing is, though, his barber knew.
Since there was no one he could tell
and keep his life, the barber went out in a field one night.
He dug a hole deep, deep enough for planting,
then got down on his knees and hung his head down low.
He laughed and let his tongue wag,
then shoveled the dirt back in the hole.
The story goes: in time, grass grew out of that soil
and whispered the story over and over again
until some shepherds heard it.
Midas became a laughing stock.

As if the grass was one thing and not fescue, zoysia,
Bermuda, bluestem, saw grass, buffalo grass, reeds,
and many other cousins that include wheat and rice and rye and corn.

Tall grasses with roots that go down twice as deep as the grave
compete with their shallow kin for their place alongside chickweed, henbit,
clover, Queen Anne's lace, wild violets, dandelions…
If the whole field, if the prairie, the marshes, what grows in the parks,
on the gridiron, the diamond, the dunes,
if all of them shouted together in chorus
who could hear them over birdsong and crickets?
I listen and I can hear only the wind's chuckle
push through dry stalks.
Not one of the grasses would say
if Midas was hiding the horns of a stag
or hair coiled like so many black snakes.
No, grass is what covers up all our messes.
Home to those that crawl and scurry,
it feeds our cattle and sheep.

Nothing stays secret for long but you can't blame the grass.
Burn it if you will, it will only grow back and be greener
than the straw and beige and grey colors of this landscape.
Be grateful it keeps sand from blowing in our eyes.
Remember it keeps the earth from eroding.
We need the ground under our feet
so we will have somewhere to stand.

THE ROAD TO HELL IS PAVED
WITH GOOD INTENTIONS

Sure, I threw some gravel down.
Mud was a problem.
But paving wasn't my idea.
What did I care
if sinners said the way was bumpy?
They wanted comfort
and they managed it.

Investors did this
—four lanes one way—
and they collect a toll
here at the gate.
For my own amusement,
I posted a speed limit.
It slows no one down.
Everyone knows once they arrive they'll burn
and scream in pain eternally.
People can't seem to get here
fast enough.

PEOPLE WHO LIVE IN GLASS HOUSES SHOULDN'T THROW STONES

I'm not the chunk of quartz you threw to scare the homeless man.
That one has blood on it.

I am a fist sized piece of granite
chosen for heft from what lined a flower bed.
Carried here and hurled,
I am still dizzy and throbbing from my journey
through your plate glass window.

The noise it made! And shattered glass everywhere!
Shocking the difference between the warm of your den
and the cold outside, though it grows less every moment.

You don't look at me.
You stare into the dark,
overcome by the weight, by the number,
by the sizes and shapes of the rocks that litter this world.

WEDDED VIRTUES

Cleanliness will not tell you
how close she is to Godliness;
she doesn't need to talk.
They have been together for so long.
Their children have grown up
and made names for themselves.

She is wise enough to know
she could be making the bed one morning
and find a long dark hair on a sheet so white it glows.

As much as she trusts her husband,
sometimes Cleanliness thinks about Charity,
the way she reaches out to everyone,
how when she meets Godliness
she hugs him or squeezes his arm.

She is affectionate, that one.
Even Godliness can be tempted.

Cleanliness will be the first to tell you that things change.

Some things you learn too late, or
—if you are lucky, nearly too late—
that it is dark chocolate, not apples,
that keeps the doctor away,
that slow and steady isn't allowed on the race track,
and what doesn't kill you
—which used to make you stronger—¬makes you fat.

DON'T PUT ALL YOUR EGGS IN ONE BASKET

Because if you drop it, they will all break.

Because your basket isn't big enough.
Balance them the best you can,
some will still roll off.

Because the basket you're using is too deep.
The weight of egg on egg on egg
will crush the shells.
Yolk will ooze through the weave on the bottom.

Because foxes can smell
all those eggs in one place.

Lucky for you, I have two baskets left
—one round, one square—
I am willing to sell.

A ROLLING STONE GATHERS NO MOSS

Even the side of you that faces the sun
will stay moist if you do not move.
Moisture means moss will grow on you,
breaking you down. Soon you'll grow soft and swell,
gradually turning to muck.

So keep moving,
even though movement grinds you down.
Bouncing against other surfaces
chips off your edges,
makes you grow smaller.
Soon, all of what used to be you
is dust on a windshield,
dirt on the sole of a sandal,
mud clinging to roots.

ROBBING PETER TO PAY PAUL

Sooner or later, you will go to answer the doorbell
and find a police officer standing on your stoop.

He'll tell you charges have been brought.
You will sit in the back of his cruiser
while he drives you to the station.
You will post bail and go home.

Things will go on as normal
for weeks, maybe months,
but, sooner to later,
you will have to go to court.

Forced to testify,
you'll clear your throat
and try to remember all the times
you took scissors from the gift wrapping station
to cut open a box,
times you took a pen from someone's desk
to sign for a package,
times you stayed late at work
while your family sat home wondering
why you hadn't come home for dinner,
how you rushed out of the house
during the party to get ice from the store
without telling anyone where you'd gone.

Sooner or later,
before you're found guilty, I hope,
you will pay Peter back,
put two pens back where you took one,
get home early, take your family out to dinner,
and tell that bastard Paul that he can go to hell.

DIG YOUR WELL BEFORE YOU ARE THIRSTY

Not that the creek is dry,
but you've pretended long enough that day won't come.
What you dip out of it is two parts sand.

Time to decide where you will want that hole
and how to make it with the least amount of work.
Near the house would be good
but right now what's important
is that you find where water is near the surface.

Once you have picked a place,
gather your tools—a shovel, a bucket,
a coil of rope, a metal bar long enough
to lay over the mouth and throw the rope across.

Next, put your gloves on. Grab the shovel.
Push the blade in. Kick it loose and lift.
Don't try to work too fast.
You'll be at this a while.

In four days or five you might strike water.
By then, you will be used to being stiff and tired.
You will be used to being in the throat
of what you're digging.

You won't admit the hours of working in the dark
make you think maybe you are going blind.
Filling the bucket up with dirt, pulling the rope
to take it to the surface, will become automatic.

When you find your boots and socks are soaked,
that water is rising to your knees,
you will—at first—be furious.

BETTER A BIRD IN THE HAND
THAN TWO IN THE BUSH

As long as you aren't afraid he will scratch his way free.
Hold tight,
even if your knuckles get pecked.
Get some water boiling.
Be ready to pluck all those feathers.

Better a bird in the hand…if you're hungry.
If your belly is full you don't mind it so much
when the sparrows flit out of the boxwood
and disappear into the sky.

THE PROVERB OF THE TOOLBOX

This morning a man I work with told me
"If your only tool is a hammer,
you will treat every problem like a nail."
I thought of that on the way home
as I marveled at a song on the radio,
wondering how they knew to use an accordion for this part
and to add horns at the end of the chorus.
Now, before I eat dinner, I will gather my tools up
from the four corners of the garage
—scissors and pliers, shovels and long-handled rakes—
and remind myself of the use for each of them.

DON'T COUNT YOUR CHICKENS
BEFORE THEY HATCH

Because I am always getting ahead of myself,
I am not even thinking about the world's best fried chicken anymore.
I'm thinking about the sides that go with it

—potatoes, corn, string beans, cole slaw, what else?
In my head, I have sold the franchising rights.

I have made millions selling the feathers for hats
and more millions stuffing pillows
with the less attractive feathers.

In our daydreams, we don't consider the cost of feed,
the price of lumber to build chicken coops, land to build them on,
the time it takes to pluck them, much less the noise,

the smell, the vet bills,
the aggravation of dealing with the pecking order.

Until they hatch, let me count them as eggs.
One boiled. Two sunny side up,
three for an omelet, four for a cake,

A dozen lined up two by two
in this neat little carton.

NO PAIN, NO GAIN

The truth is that not every proverb
is good advice.
Ask anyone with a hernia
or a torn rotator cuff.
Ask the man living on ramen noodles
because he went all in with an investment.
Someone had told him,
"In for a penny, in for a pound."
No possum. No sup. No taters.
No shoes, no shirt, no service.
See no evil. Hear no evil…
 No, no, no. No, no. No.

IF THE SHOE FITS...

If I walked a mile in another man's moccasins,
maybe I'd learn not to judge him so harshly.
More likely, I would wear a blister on my toe.
They say the wearer knows where the boot pinches.
I say she should know when to take it off.
I know it is none of my business
but her heels are higher than her cigarette is long.

Who could help looking at her?
Who could help thinking
those stilettos proclaim the quality of her legs
the same way smoking celebrates her breath?

AFTER SHOUTING AT A STRANGER, "I COULD STILL BEAT YOUR ASS, SONNY!"

I bite my tongue.
No one should have to tell me
not to climb up on my roof to show my wife I can,
not to drive when I've had five beers,
not to pick a fight in the parking lot of Walmart.

How did I come to do all three things
on a Wednesday night?

To learn from my mistakes
I would have to remember why
my jaw hurts and my collarbone
and that other people suffer
from things I have done.

This fresh ache in my toes will remind me
not to kick a barstool for a while
but even I have figured out
pain is not wisdom.

THE SQUEAKY WHEEL GETS THE GREASE

It is only when you lower your window
that you hear it
and you aren't sure what you hear.

At first, you tell yourself it is the wind,
a creaky door,
maybe the fan belt of a passing car.
You find yourself driving around the block
to listen for it.

Over time, it grows louder
and more shrill.
It sets your teeth on edge.
You wish the squeaking was articulate,
that it would proclaim
what it is, where it comes from.

Finally, you put your car up on a lift
and find the wheel that drags when it goes round.
It is easy enough to fix.
You squeeze grease where metal rubs metal
until it spins smoothly, quietly.

But what is this lubricant, exactly?
No longer rendered fat.
Some chemicals are blended together
for the right viscosity,
a stickiness to free up friction
that catches fuzz and sand
and God knows what else.

A LITTLE KNOWLEDGE IS A DANGEROUS THING

Lucky for us, I don't know enough Spanish
to think you are demanding my keys
when you offer me eggs.

But if I were to learn your language
I would have to start somewhere,
for a time comprehending imperfectly
what you are saying.
The things I get wrong
will confuse what I do understand
until my mistakes are corrected.

Measuring knowledge
in powder form or liquid,
by the teaspoon or the liter,
how do I know when the mark has been reached
to signify mastery?
Or, to put it more simply,
how much is a little?

THIS ONE COMES WITH A SCAR

(haste makes waste)

Sliced open my finger early this morning
cutting up onions to go in my eggs.
Wasted a bunch a paper towels.
Had to hold my hand over my head
to get it to stop bleeding.
Washed it. Dabbed it with ointment.
Wrapped a band aid around it.
Had to wipe up the blood on the counter.
All this put me behind.

Though I was hurrying to work,
I noticed you, Barbara, pacing your driveway,
cell phone to your ear.
You had locked your keys in the house
and were calling Jack to come let you in.
You, Ryan, I saw on the shoulder of the highway.
You'd failed to check the needle on your gas gauge.
Kate, I saw you, frantic, retracing your steps.
You'd left your wallet on the grocery store counter.

Since I woke up this morning I've been making mistakes,
or, maybe, at last, I've recognized
when I am doing things wrong.

Now, when I should be keeping my eyes
on the car in front of me,
I see all of you who are limping
because you didn't take the time
to look where you were going,
each one of you who has an arm in a cast,
every single person who has to take a minute
or three to get out of his chair
because of that injury from weeks or months or years ago.
No, we haven't met, but I know you.

More than those I see at church on Sunday
or twice a week at the gym, more than my own family,
more than the other guys who go out on their kayaks,
more than the few of us who revere the name Virginia Hamilton Adair,
I know you. I know all about you. You are my people.

2. Bible Stories

THE FRUIT OF GOOD, THE FRUIT OF EVIL

The trees were there all along, at first white with blooms,
then green with leaves.
In time, the fruit grew so heavy on the boughs
it dragged down the branches.
The apples were ripe in October when Eve found the tree.
The sweet reek of the rotten ones soft on the ground,
the red orbs, the snake's whisper.
How long did she hesitate before she plucked the apple
and bit through the skin to white flesh?
Had Eve wiped the juice from her chin before she felt the chill
of winter and realized she was naked?
Since then, life has been work.

Naked and cold, she gripped the first apple,
great grandma of the Granny Smith, the Macintosh,
the Golden, the Gala, the Stayman,
all the varieties that fry up well, that hold together
when you bake them, sliced in pies, cored in dumplings,
the ones that fall apart for apple sauce, apple butter, jelly.
You could hold in one hand the bruised and lumpy mass
that fell on Newton's head
and in the other the candy red perfection
(marred only with the oval dent of teeth)
that put Snow White to sleep.

Whatever shape or color, they are sweet
in a world that is bitter for many.

Bring the ladders, the baskets. It is apple-picking time.
There are people with stories they only tell in winter,
when there is leisure to hear them.
Now it is time for the hard labor of gathering to put away.
There are places where they ask, "How is work?"
And the answer is always the same, "I am grateful for it."

RAIN-SOAKED SHIRT

I remember a promise God made once the ark came to rest,
a covenant not with a man or a people but with all living flesh
—with tigers in Asia, with African lions,
Indian elephants, monkeys in Brazil,
with doves and with ravens and the hens that lay our eggs.

To my dog and to my neighbor's cat,
to me and you and the mouse in his hole
God made this promise:
though there will be downpours and flooding,
though some will be soaked to the bone
and many will drown,

the Almighty will not use the rain to destroy us,
to cover the earth, to silence all breath.

It is no small thing.

A RAM CAUGHT BY ITS HORNS
IN THE BRAMBLES

I was young enough to be excited, even proud,
that Father Abraham would take me
on the journey to meet his god.

When we came to the mountain,
we left the men and the donkeys behind.
I carried the firewood.

Climbing, I was afraid
to ask questions, then I was scared not to,
when we stopped and he uncoiled the rope.

Pausing to watch my own sons tussle,
I lean on my staff
and feel a tug in my shoulders

from so many years ago. when I shrieked for mercy
as he twisted my arms behind my back
and tied my wrists.

I couldn't take my eyes off
the knife on the ground
by the blaze he had started.

How long did we listen to that creature's braying
before my father went to claim him,
waiting until the beast was secure
before he came back
to loosen the knots he'd tied?

TWO BLESSINGS

I want the rain to be your friend,
trembling the leaves of your tomato plants.
I want its rhythm to fill your songs.

Thirsty, may you swallow all you want.
On hot, cloudless days, may you splash out
and swim in the cool, dark deep.

But more than that, I want you be like Esau,
who, when offered flocks of goats and sheep
by the brother who had cheated him,

was able to refuse Jacob's gift.
Though he lived far from the dew of Heaven,
though it was so dry his tongue stuck to his teeth,

he could embrace his twin. He could say,
"I have enough."

SOMBRERO

Frosting was running down the back of my neck.
I took a clump of cake from under the band of my hat,
from just over my eyes, to taste it.
Such rich fudge icing! But the yellow cake was stale,
hard to choke down. Crumbs blew in the wind.

I wiped my mouth with my sleeve. My throat was dry.
 I looked for fountains, for buildings, for booths.
 There was nothing to drink anywhere.
I crossed the beach toward the ocean,
meaning to wade in, to wash the mess out of my hair,
but before I could reach the waves
I heard flapping wings and felt a bird light on my crown.
I waved my arms, but failed to frighten it.

Next, gulls flew circles around me.
The brim of my hat was so broad
I couldn't see them when they came close.
I couldn't reach them to smack them away.
My head shook when the birds pecked at the cake.
They looped sideways with bits in their beaks.

I spun around to dislodge them, but that made me dizzy.
I tried to run on the sand
while gulls were pinching the flesh of my arms, of my neck.
Their cries grew insistent. Their bills turned to scissors and knives.
Lightheaded, I screamed but nobody heard over their shrieking.
Now nothing is felt, nothing heard, but I watch everything.

Through the skin of things on earth I see joints rubbing together.
I look up and see how things are spread out on the sky
—hot dishes, cold dishes—
where that broad tablecloth is stained,
the way it's creased where it was folded,
and how it's covered with a lacey pattern made of tiny holes.

BIG SISTER

It was you, Miriam,
who stole the grain basket.
You coated its bottom and sides
so it would float,

then filled it with straw
so your brother's bottom
wouldn't stick to the tar.

You toted Moses back and forth
to his mother for milk.
Holding him by the wrists,
you dipped his body in the river
to clean him off.

You worried he would float away,
that a crocodile would eat him,
marveled at his tiny wrinkled fingers.

When the princess came to bath
and found the baby,
you stepped out of the reeds
and offered to find a nurse.

Did no one in the entourage notice
your legs were wet,
or that there was mud
 in a ring around your hem?

LAMB

A dark smear
around the frame of my door.
I pick at it with my thumbnail.
It's blood.

I get a pail of water,
soap, and a sponge,
but, coming outside,
I see the house across the street
has also been marked.

Stepping out into the yard,
I look left and right.
Some of the doorframes are painted,
smeared, with blood. Some are not.

Somewhere, meat is grilling.
I try to follow my nose
but lose the scent.
It's almost dusk.

About to turn back,
I spot a father and son
on their porch,
scrubbing their doorposts clean.

The father sees me,
comes down the steps,
 shakes his head,
Looking over his shoulder,
he says. "Strange things are happening."
He asks, "What does this mean?"

NO PATH BUT GOD

You may long to go home, home to Jehovah.
You may believe that you are Moses
with the desert in front of you,
but while God made a path through the sea
he made no path here.

By day, the Deity you follow is a cloud.
By night, God is a flame.
Time and again, you cross tracks you have worn.
When you choose a place or when God picks one for you,
will that piece of ground be your home?

The angels eternally sweep and sing
but there's so much Promised Land in Heaven,
you will feel grit underfoot on the floor.

SAMUEL

The beginning of wisdom is knowing right names for things,
knowing when to speak them, knowing when to listen for your own.
A woman opens the front door of her house
and cries out into the darkness the names of her children.
The words echo off the buildings
and down the street to where they are playing a game.
It is summer, so it's not time for dinner. It's time for bed.
When they come in they are surprised
at how dark the world looks through the windows.
Necessities, pleasures, opportunities, distractions,
summon, request, demand your attention
as if it was a little thing.
It is the only thing that is really your own.
The bell that is chiming, to you it is only noise, only music.
Once, it called you to prayer.

ZIG ZAG

Dry, bleached white, they covered the floor of the valley.
How they came there,
what disaster met those people, is not recorded.
All we know is Ezekiel preached to their bones and they responded to the Word
of God.
Parts that had been splintered, pitted, Parts that had been ground into dust.
Worked free of the sand and dirt. Took their old shapes, became whole.
Tibias, kneecaps, femurs, jaws, skulls, The small bones of the hands and feet,
Disks of the back, humerus, radius—all separated by vultures picking them
apart, by wolves, dogs, rodents, gravity, and rain-found each other, joint to
socket, rattled together,
became green, marrowed, somehow, bound up with sinews, muscle, skin, as the
prophet called for breath that they might live.
They marched, naked, across the desert, away from muttering Ezekiel,
not even knowing they would need water and food.
The new skin on their shoulders was pink within minutes.
All of them were children, even the wrinkled ones
who stroked their beards, squeezed their limbs.
They were afraid that in the haste of creation
some bones had been confused, women's with men's,
that specks of grass or bits of bugs had been swept up and lodged
in their bodies before skin grew to cover them,
that parts of them might be the horns of cattle or the teeth of dogs,
that—even from the beginning—they weren't pure.

STRAIGHT AND NARROW

Roads are made crooked to follow the world.

That one twists around Afton Mountain.
This one swerves to link Chesapeake to Portsmouth
on its way to Norfolk's docks.
Nine out of ten turn so they won't cross a river.
The tenth road will cross this river and nine more.

The ladder you'll climb up to heaven is straight.
Its rungs are even.
This ladder won't sway in the wind.
It won't teeter through earthquakes.
Hand over hand, you will rise through the brightening sky.

People will see you and pull off the road.
On the shoulder of the interstate
they will get out of their cars and turn their faces up
to see you—so small overhead, barely a speck.
They will squint, shading their eyes with their hands,
oblivious to the traffic blowing by,
though the wind it stirs up tugs at their clothes.

When your neck aches from craning
and your legs are wobbly,
when the itch between your shoulder blades
needs to rub against something,
you will wonder about changing directions
and climbing back down, but, sucking thin air,
you will keep going. You will go until you drop,
until you tumble into grace,
until you fall into God's breast pocket.

BLASPHEMY

It is the greatest of sins
unless you don't believe
and then it is merely bad manners.

But what of the man
who only thinks he has lost his faith?

He says he is a wolf
who chewed off his own leg to be free
of the trap that was his faith.

What he does not tell you
is the mangled foot he left behind
itches like crazy.

GOOD MORNING

When the alarm went off
I stumbled to the bathroom,
felt for the light.

Head hung over the sink,
I poured water into my cupped hand,
rubbed my face.

Looking into the mirror,
I wet my curls,
smoothed down my cowlick.

Now I am fumbling in the drawer
past nail files, scissors, bandages,
for something to work out these tangles.

If there is a God,
a God right here,
who knows the number of hairs on my head,

even this plastic comb is sacred.

LENT: GIVING UP SUGAR FOR A WHILE

I try not to think about
how young Jesus was

when he gave up
writing in the dirt with his finger,

when he gave up making mud
 of his spit to cure the blind,

the legs that carried him everywhere,
eyesight, hearing, smell and taste,

the ability to swallow,
his breath moving in and out,

his heartbeat,
the heat at the core of his body.

SUSTENANCE

Christ did not cheapen himself
by becoming bread and wine.
No, the cup is holy
and the plate and knife and fork.

Don't think so much wheat and corn grows on stalks,
so many apples and pears hang from boughs,
so many potatoes and turnips and carrots root in the earth,
that people don't starve.

Will only the dogs get your scraps?
Will only the ants get your crumbs?
Who might you feed?

What you eat becomes part of you,
fueling the swing of your arms,
your hips' wiggle, your grin.

Give praise for the bowl. Praise the spoon
you mold your mouth around.
Revere the stove, the oven,
the brass pan, the iron skillet.

The farmer, the grocer, the waitress,
do they serve you
or are they servants of what they bring you?

Savor.
Marvel at this soup: the onion, the celery, the pepper.
It tastes better, doesn't it, now that you're hungry?
Food should be shared.

Remember you are kin to what you eat.
Even the yeast in this loaf
had a life of its own.

3. This Life

VICTUALS AND SPEECH

The lungs and the belly
fork off the same passage
because food and talk go together.
They are ways that we express ourselves.

Either can choke you
or nourish you.
There is texture to both.

Consider how cuisines and languages
perish in tandem,
leaving no corpses.

Both are learned in the kitchen,
not in the dining room.
A feast or a nibble.
A word or a story.

The hot. The sweet. The bitter.
Forgotten as quickly
as you lick them off your teeth.

In my family, we make a paste
of vinegar and sugar to put on our waffles.
We eat pickled peaches.

Here, take this in your mouth.
It is something Po Pop used to say:

If you look for flowers,
you'll find flowers.
If you look for weeds,
you'll find weeds.

Push that around with your tongue.

LOCAL

Once any native of this place
shelled her own beans and shucked the corn she ate,
reached up and plucked an apple off a tree
to sink her teeth into.
Your bones and your flesh were formed
out of the produce of the local gardens.
Your richness came from soil,
from what was underfoot.
Your muscles were as much the evidence of dung-rich soil
as of the effort used to sow the harvest.
Your plumpness testified to frequent rains.
Now your food comes from other places,
your cheese from distant cows. Even your water is imported.
You took your first breathe here
but air comes and goes with the wind.
You walk our streets, but most of them are paved
with stones that came as ballast
from one of a thousand foreign ports.
Say what you will, as long as you chew your macaroons,
sip Guatemalan coffee, swill French wine,
peel California oranges,
and load your fork with sea bass from Chile
or beef from Japan,
you're not from here.

A TALE OF THE FAMINE

The children believed the old woman
who talked about Hansel and Gretel.

Their mouths watered when she spoke
of a gingerbread house.

She lingered over the part
where Hansel was imprisoned and fed.

The witch would tell him,
"Stick out your finger."

So she could feel
if he was plump enough to eat.

He would hold out a bone
he had found in his cell.

Stunted listeners imagined feasting
'til even their hands grew fat.

WHAT GOT ME HERE

So many ways to cover ground.
Stroll. Hike. Trot.
On tip toe. Leaping.
Over grass. Over rocks.

 I stand in one place,
shift my weight
from one leg to another,
from my heels to the balls of my feet.

It is only when I stumbled
that I noticed how little space
was between my sole
and a tuft of grass, a fallen branch.

This half of my body moves me.
Up from my toenails
through the arches
of my feet, ankles, shins,
the hollow behind the knees,
 the long muscles of my thighs
leading up to my sex,
the crack of my butt,
my hip's ball and socket.

This is why I can sit, stand, straddle,
why I can get down on my knees.
These bones, these joints, push the pedals
on my car, turns the gears on my bike.

Now I have kicked the door shut
behind me, I'm grateful.
And when I found myself dodging trees
as I raced through the woods,
I was glad
most of my power was in my legs,
even before I knew
what I was running from.

NITROGEN

I do not claim to be the atmosphere
but I am most of it.

Oxygen will set paper smoking,
burn your house down.

I am the stable one,
holding up clouds and planes and kites.

Birds, bats, and insects
wing their way through me.

Whatever blows in the wind
is interspersed with me.

Whichever direction you turn,
I press against your face.

Whatever it is you need when you breathe,
I am what fills your lungs.

AN ARGUMENT FOR STAYING PUT

We don't talk about the mania that drove us here
or reminisce about that other country.
In no time we've convinced ourselves
such a disruption won't happen again.
Next time we'll hiss and honk at whoever suggests
leaves turning red or gold means the foliage will drop.
We will remind them it is not leaves we subsist on.

We had no reason to fly in the path of men with guns
who wobbled to their feet to shoot at us,
eagerly rising from long grass
or nearly swamping the boats where they waited
to point the long barrels and blow holes in the air.

Plainly, they'd been tipped off to where
we were going and when it was we'd leave.
Weeks it took and all that time we were sore
from flying hours a day and from sleeping
in parking lots, too tired half the time
to get out of the way of the cars.

Though to some who live here we will always be outsiders
we have made a place for ourselves on the lake.
There are enough of us and we are big enough
we feel comfortable,
at home on this land, in this sky,
and, mainly, in this water where we drift and doze.
The heat makes us sluggish
or maybe it is stuffing ourselves that brings on this stupor.

—

A few months later we were good and used to it.
We had learned or remembered where things are,
accepting, at last, this was not a new place after all.
Then, for no reason, I grew restless.
The cacophony of birds and insects singing over each other
was the same as it was before except it got under my skin.
The heat might have bothered me. Thinking back, it's hard to tell.

I noticed a friend or two had gone missing
from a place with no predators but I said nothing.

Today I gathered myself and lumbered up into the blue.
With the weight I've gained, it wasn't easy to reach this height.
It's painful, but there is no use in wondering what draws me.
A few miles out I see a pond and swoop down for a drink.
Only now, as I settle in mud in the shade of a bridge,
do I notice the geese setting down here and there on my flanks,
three in the water, two in the clearing behind me…
only now do I stretch up my neck
and discover how we line the sky.

THE PIETY OF THE ARTIFICIAL

Because I am your priest, I hear your confessions,
What you say individually, what you recite in unison.

Air handler, you raise your voice in the hallway.

"I envy your softness
and the way your muscles move beneath your skin.
Explain to me: bruises, wiggle, recline.
I know it is sin to covet
but I want what you have,
I want flesh."

Siri, I pick up my phone and you ask me:

"What is it to hunger?
What is it to have hunger satisfied?"
I can't begin to explain., I've memorized your prayer. It goes,
"Your sweat fascinates me.
I repent of my envy and then there it is again.
What shall I do?"

Laptop, each morning you bow down in front of me
and whisper:

"If your feet were mine
they would strike the ground hard as I ran.
My knees would rise high as my hipbone.
My elbows would flash."

From my car, from my kitchen,
wherever I go,
you devices are raising your voices.
I pity you all,
since from every direction I hear:

"I want spit in my mouth
and mucus to moisten my nose."

"I want to make water.
I want a reason to squat."

"I watch you rub against each other,
squeeze, cling, hold.
I long to feel and I am ignorant of touch.
What does it mean to kiss?
What does it mean to embrace?"

You are certain that humans' complaints—
the pain of a bee sting,
disgust at the stench of old fish,
the weariness of work with no sleep—
would be, to you, wonderfully visceral.

I cannot program you
or teach you what you are not meant to know,
but I can lead you in worship,
give you the word, assign penance.

I celebrate you before the Creator.
I raise you up before the Lord.

SKIN

The tongue and the lungs make themselves heard.
The stomach grumbles. The nose sniffs.
The eyes show you pictures.
Ears bring you noise.

I tell you when you've stepped on a nail
in a board in your attic,
when you've sliced your thumb cutting a bagel,
when it's too cold to stay outside.

Pain. Discomfort.
Touch has many pleasures but you need it most
to know your lips are chapped from licking them,
your ankle itches where the mosquito bit you,
that you scraped your arm against a brick wall.

Again and again I tell you: be more careful.

While the heart, the liver, the kidneys
do their easy business inside,
who sweats for you as you mow the yard?
Who goes gooseflesh when the temperature drops?
Who endures the heat of August,
the cold of February?

Who forms calluses on your hands,
grows thick on the soles of your feet,
on your elbows?

 It's what I do so you're protected
when you grab a bar bell or a tree branch,
stride barefoot across gravel,
when you crawl to retrieve a fork
or a shoe or a child.

The scars, bumps, wrinkles that I have
show what we've been through.

Stretched over your frame,
I keep what's inside clean.

Loose enough so you can move,
tight enough I don't get pinched
the way your clothes get caught on fences,
on the arms of chairs and in car doors.

You love the sun on your shoulders
but hate sunburn.
You scratch with your nails
what is damaged already, what peels.

I need someone else to rub me,
to pat, to stroke, to squeeze.
Can you reach out in a way
that won't get me slapped?
Can you do that for me?

PERRY MASON

The accused seems guilty.
He can't explain why he went to see the victim
that night between midnight and three a.m.,

how his gun went from his bedside table
to the middle drawer of the dead man's desk,

why he came back to California now
after years in Brazil.

A woman testifies she saw his car speed away.
His boss admits he caught him in a lie.
His father blames himself for spoiling his son.

No one is sorry the murdered man is dead.
He was a bully, a letch, a blackmailer.

By the second commercial, you suspect
the uncut diamonds in the safety deposit box
are really rock candy,

the fifty dollar bill rolled in the window blind
is part of the haul from the bank robbery.

That con man is the skipper from *Gilligan's Island*.
That weasel is Murray from *Mary Tyler Moore*.

In each episode, Lt. Tragg glowers at our hero.
Hamilton Burger protests that Mason's questions
are irrelevant, impertinent, and immaterial.

The murderer always confesses,
either in the witness box or from the gallery.

How we hunger for story,
even if it's the same one every time.

COMING FROM A FLAT LAND

Pale humps appeared in the distance.
They vanished as I descended toward a bridge.
Coming into view again, each time a brighter blue.

In and out of tree shade on the winding two lane,
the roofs of old barns and abandoned houses,

the slopes of mountains,
each steeper than the one before.

This one bashed in. That one buckled.
None of them square.

Speeding down the far side of one of those peaks,
I saw a wide bare path

made for trucks that lose their brakes.
I tried not to think about
how much I had used my right foot.

The scenery below the guard rail was all stripes and spots, stained
by the shadows of clouds.

Finally, the driveway to my sister's house.
Turning the wheel, I hit the gas, and climbed.

Parked on a slant,
I stepped down to get out,
pushed the car door up to slam it.

Walking sideways, ascending,
 my ankles stretched as my toes pointed.
The muscles of my thighs
 clutched at my knees.

Aware, for once,
of how my body struggles against gravity,

I threw my shoulders back.

The ground reared up,
 taunting my smallness.

Lightheaded, I planted my feet
and forced myself to stand straight.

YOU'VE GOT TO MOVE

There is nothing wrong with buying a new chair
or softer sheets, nothing wrong
with adding a screened in porch to your house.

But life will be cramped
if you feel out of place beyond your threshold,
if your only sanctuary is your bed.

When you prepare to leave on your journey,
don't pack too much or your shoulders will ache.
Don't wear the shoes that rub blisters.

Go where the natives go.
Try new foods, new drink.
Learn to be grateful for shade.

To be at home in the world,
you will need to cross borders.
Turned away at the gate, you'll have no choice

but to get down below the barbed wire.
Crawling on your belly,
lift your chin. Keep your mouth shut.
Who wants to be spitting out sand?

NO ONE WILL EVER BE THIS CLOSE TO ME

You lift my shirttail
and plunge upward

till you head emerges
through my collar.

Your arms are under mine.
The fabric stretches

as we rearrange ourselves.
Breathing together,

our smells mingle.
It is a wonder

our legs don't tangle.
It is a wonder

that leaning into each other
we stay on our feet.

WHAT IS FORGOTTEN BECOMES NEW

So much was familiar:
the bones of the mosasaur
which coiled overhead as we entered,
the bees on the sixth floor
that we watched travel from the hive
through a tube to fly out over the roof,

examples of taxidermy: elk, bears, hawks,
skulls with antlers, fossils, so much,
but how could I have forgotten
florescent shark teeth
and these rocks that glow brightly
—blue, green, yellow—in the dark?

The first time we were here
this velvet ant with her dusty hindquarters
must have been in this glass case near the floor.
Here it says she is really a wasp
with four times the venom of a bee.
Called the cow killer,
no one would forget her sting.

THE POVERTY OF COMPLIMENTS

"Adorable" is what you call children.
It is a little condescending.
"Cute" on the other hand,
is how you describe a child
who has lost a front tooth.

"Pretty" means good bones.
It doesn't describe her expression,
the way her smile lights up a room.
"Beautiful" is for landscapes,
and, maybe, for flowers.

Call her "graceful"
and she will become self-conscious
about every move she makes.

"Smart" isn't something he'll believe.
Hearing it, he will start avoiding what is hard.
That is, unless he thinks you are praising guile,
admiring him for being crooked.

"Skinny" only works when it's not accurate.
To the terribly thin, it's insulting.

"Nice"—that means stupid, doesn't it?
Or was I thinking of "brave?"

"Hard working"—well,
that is recognition of something
besides talent. "Talented" means
"Good for you for being lucky."

Are there others I should know about,
Things I can say that won't be taken wrong?

I didn't think so.

It is kind of you to listen.

WAKING UP LUCKY

I fling myself against the seat back,
somehow not swerving.
My eyes water.

Broken lines strobe in my headlights.
The drone of my tires.
A moon stabbed by trees.

I wipe my mouth
with fingers and the back of my hand,
check in the mirror that my face is clean.

My nose throbs where it hit the steering wheel.
Has the bleeding's stopped?
I sniff. Warm metal runs down my throat.

Beside me, you snore in the passenger seat.
Your mouth is open. The road curves left
after running straight so long.

When the sun comes up and you stretch and turn,
what will I say when you ask
why blood darkens the front of my shirt?

WHEN WE PAID OFF THE MORTGAGE

I opened my closets
and said to my clothes, "You can stay."

I announced to the furniture,
"You won't have to move again."

I wandered the house,
banging my knuckles against the walls,

running my fingers along the counters,
bending down to put my palms

flat on the cool hardwood floor.
Mine.   Mine.   Mine.

That's what I did yesterday.
Now, outside, it's time to put away my tools

after power washing mold off bricks,
mowing grass, trimming hedges.

I push myself to a stand after leaning on you, pin oak.
I step back and look up at your height

from the shade you cast.
How can it be that I own you?

Could I own the cloud above us,
or the rain that is starting to fall?

AS THEIR TONGUES SHAPE THE NAME OF GOD

The air in heaven cannot be so thin
it will not carry odor.

When angel choirs exhale their songs of praise
they fill their noses as their fill their lungs
with scents of sandalwood, leather, fresh brewed coffee,
line-dried linen, roses, the tang of pine, lime's tickle, mint….

Here below, bumblebees stir the heat with their wings.
Shade dapples the yard.
Though I am an old man
—wheezing as I pull the long, tangled hose
to water the edge of the garden—
the smell of lavender blends with my blood.

A MUMBLED BLESSING

When, as an infant, you first became hungry or cold
you cried out in panic.
Given a tit to suck, wrapped in a blanket,
you didn't feel gratitude; you felt relief.

You were taught to say "Thank you." as a toddler,
years before you understood the words.
How were you supposed to know, "Don't mention it." "It's nothing."
were what people said to be polite.
Not that they gave you things in order to be thanked,
but grown-ups need their gifts to be recognized.

Sometimes what we see as ingratitude
is a difference in etiquette or a difference in standards.
Some tribes hold things in common
and don't understand that what is mine is not yours.
Others, like the Japanese, beg pardon when we would give thanks
because they feel the weight of debt so keenly.

Bread in my mouth is tasteless if I don't acknowledge
it does more than fill a hole. Time must be taken to give thanks,
to praise the earth the wheat was rooted in, the hands that kneaded,
the oven's heat, the God that made the teeth that tear it
and this tongue that takes in sour and sweet, bitter and salty,
that feels its texture, pushes it around,
this tongue that shapes so many foolish notions
but that can soothe, can warn, instruct, advise, encourage,
that can pray and sing.
I praise them not because they need these words
but because I need to say them.

I open my mouth and I'm rich.

BLUNT INSTRUMENTS

A new ax works as it should.
Chop the trunk here and here.
Bark and chips fly.
A small v grows big.
Your muscles tighten at the sound
of cracking and splintering wood.
The ground trembles
when the tree goes sideways.

But doing thing over and over again
dulls the ax
and dulls the mind
of the man who swings from the hips.

If he does not stop, now and then,
and take time to sharpen the blade,
the job gets harder and harder.

Eventually, he finds himself
trying to chop down a tree
with a hammer.

I AM THE MAN WHO YELLS AT HIS WIFE

Saying, "Bitch, I'll put a cap in your ass!"
because you asked me to repeat
what the villain said on TV.
I raise my voice to say I love you,

bellow how good you look
in your new blue blouse,
shout about the chicken enchiladas
you made for my dinner.

Tuesday, you get your new hearing aids.
Wednesday, you will know that I've come home
from the jangle of keys unlocking the door.
You will know where I am in the house

when you hear the creak of the floorboards,
water running in the shower,
the clack of hangers in the closet.
I will speak softly

and my words will be fingertips
massaging the base of your skull.
I'll whisper something in your ear
and hear the music of your laughter.

A PRAYER STITCHED TOGETHER

Somehow basil cell carcinoma didn't frighten me.
Neither did going under the knife

on Thursday to cut it away,
then to the plastic surgeon on Friday.

I am grateful for that,
even more than for none of it hurting.
When I took the white pill,

I could hear pain's hooves clomping down the street.
It stopped before it reached this house.

Who would have believed I'd be happy
there are stitches across the bridge of my nose
where my glasses always rest?

Is it because the scar will be evidence
of mornings that I fought the waves
of the Atlantic in my kayak?

Too near sighted to work, I have to take a week off.
My wife puts cold compresses on my eyes.
 She finds music I want to listen to.

For a while I will have an excuse to talk to people
and tell lies about the J shaped scar on my nose,
explaining to my mailman a loan shark
pushed me through a plate glass window....

Would I feel differently about it
if I had pulled the bandage off Thursday night
and seen the hole?

THE ASTRONAUT'S BODY

Up. Down.
Words without meaning.

I only know there's no need
to work hard to push blood to my head,

no need for these muscles, these bones.
Here, they are a burden.

I let them thin.
They flow away in my urine.

From now on, I'll float.

I can barely remember what it was like
to rise, to walk,

the effort it took
to clamor to my feet.

THE FACE ON THE CLOCK

Once even I couldn't tell
my left arm from my right.
Time confused everyone
before I bit the fingernails
of one hand down to the wrist.

Now, afraid of my hunger,
it wants to bend at the elbow
and hide behind my back.
It moves slowly. It's all I can do
to keep it straight.

BLESS THE DOCTORS' WHITE COATS

May the color, the fabric, the cut,
make those who put them on
smart, curious, ready and able to heal.
May the sight of those garments
give patients comfort.

Bless the clothes of the rest of us:
the policewoman's badge hanging crooked,
half torn from her blouse,
the big red hat of the fireman
with the crack along its crown,
the jeans the roofer peels from his body
when he gets home, stiff with tar and sweat.

If it is possible, may our shoes make us quick.
May what we pull up around our waists make us strong.
May we put on confidence as we dress for work.

Most of all, bless the flesh we have in common
beneath what we wear.
May our skin glow.
May our limbs, toes, and fingers be graceful.
May our organs and senses do what they do, joyfully.
May we be humble and gentle and kind
to the marrow of our bones.

4. Finales

SLAPPED, I JUMP OUT OF MY CHAIR

And chase you room to room,
out the door, into the street.

Outside, the house
and the neighborhood recede.

This gravel road is new to me.

You are a five year old boy
in shorts and a white T shirt.
You have a crew cut.

I fall in step with you
the best I can, barefoot.

I hop and curse
when I stub my toes
and when my heel is cut
by sharp rocks in the road.

You, too, are unshod,
but your soles are as tough
as the hooves of a goat.

You skip away from me.
I get winded
trying to keep up.

You are my future.

You are my death.

ON THE WAY TO THE NEW RIVER GORGE

we passed the spot where John Henry died,
on one of those twisty roads through the woods,
on a mountainside in West Virginia.

We didn't stop.
It was barely a clearing in front of a tunnel.

Someone might have said, "Right,
and over here is the rope Pecos Bill used to catch the cyclone."
A tunnel that size—trains were smaller then.

I find myself thinking of that place in the days
they were digging that passage.
How dirty it was, how crowded, how hot,
and how loud between the ringing steel,
the clamor and strain of the steam engine,
voices singing out encouragement,
and the echo of it all thrown back by the mountains.

When I am 93 and cold all the time,
take my by the elbow and draw me to my feet.
Help me put on shoes that aren't hospital slippers.
Take me outside.
Wrap my fingers around the long handle of a 12 pound hammer.
Remind me I'm foolish enough to think I can beat the machine,
proud and reckless enough to win the race.
Let me try to lift the weight over my head.
Who knows? I might do it.
Either way, when my heart bursts in my chest
  I'll die happy.

HERRINGBONE

I am wearing this coat
because a man I knew died.
His widow noticed I am the size that he was.

One time he told me
how he went to visit a boy he knew
on a ranch when he got back from the war.

A week later the boy's father, the rancher,
asked how he had leisure
to be out riding horses.

Tom told the man he was killing time
between roles in the movies.
He loved to tell stories.

I'm wearing this coat
because my friend died,
though it's not really cold enough yet.

SKELETON

I can't take credit for my shape.
Because you are the cup for my thoughts,

the cage for my lungs, I want to say
you are strong because I drank milk,

proclaim that no part of you will break,
assure myself that (though I can't see them)

the bones of my feet are white and shiny like my teeth,
but it is not virtue that makes my elbows sharp.

It's not my righteousness that keeps the ball of my thigh
from rubbing against the socket of my pelvis,

if I grow smug and forget to be grateful
for your design—this chain of vertebrae,

the collarbones, every piece of you unique—
may my jaw fall away from my skull.

LOWERED VOICES

1.

A month ago we buried a girl
who knew her date was drunk
when it was time to leave the party.
She got in the car with him.

The Indian boy two weeks ago
who went out on the lake
in a borrowed canoe
had never learned to swim.

There was this woman last Wednesday
who could not bear to wait
until she reached home
to answer her cell phone.

The little blonde in the box Monday
who died of what doctors could not cure
—her mother believed she was faking an illness
so she could stay home from school.

The one in all the papers—athlete, scholar—
pulled into a parking space at 7 Eleven
beside a man who was already angry.
He was shot because his music was too loud.

2.

I tell the truth in my eulogies, mainly,
but I learn more once the service is over,
finding out details too late
as people who don't often see each other
catch up on who is doing what.

Between sips of tea and bites of deviled egg,
I hear how it happened, sometimes even why.

It is easy to say this one was foolish,
that one was proud,
and not think about how lucky we have been.

3.

I mind my tongue.
I wash my hands a dozen times a day,
look both ways twice before I cross.

Lately, I find myself making sure
my right heel touches down
before my left toe leaves the floor.

I am right to be careful.
I stand at the soft edge of an open grave,
dizzy and ready to fall.

WASHING THE STAINS OF HELL
FROM DANTE'S FACE

The rushes Virgil used to scrub soot from the poet's cheek
were natives of Tuscany.
Each locale in the Inferno, Purgatorio,
even the book on Heaven,
were Italian as opera, as biscotti, as pointy toed shoes.
No matter that Dante was an exile. In his head the map of his home
intertwined with the map of his body.
Wherever he was,
his tongue would remind him that the plum tomatoes
were not as sweet as those grown back in Lucca,
his eyes, his skin, that the sun's rays where he stood came down
at a different angle than they did in Florence.
How could it be otherwise?

SAINT POPS

The faded sky you keep in the window frame
is not the blue of the big sky,
not the color Louis Armstrong was looking at
when he put his horn to his lips
and his eyes rolled back in his head,
not the blue of the reverberating heaven
where Louis plays now,
where the angels join the hot five on the chorus,
and every saint listens for the cue to start a solo,
some playing clarinets, some trombones,
drums, banjos, tubas, guitars, and pianos.
God taps his foot and nods his head.
Everybody is grinning—brighter than halos.
Everybody does the sugar foot strut
and everybody gets their chance to shake the sky
in loud, loud heaven.

Additional Acknowledgments

The poem "I am the Man Who Yells at His Wife" won the Golden Quill Award from Devil's Party Press and was featured in their anthology What Sort of Fuckery is This? "The Piety of the Artificial" won the award for best poem in praise of technology in one of the Poetry Society of Virginia's contests in 2017.

In 2018, "Big Sister" won first place in the Poetry Society of Virginia's Brodie Herndon Memorial contest. In 2019, his winners in that society's contests were "A Ram Caught in the Brambles," first prize in the Loretta Dunn Hall Memorial, and "What is Forgotten Becomes New," first prize in the Laura Day Boggs Memorial.

Bill Ayres would like to thank Gayle, his wife, his life, his muse; his family, all those who have taught him at Virginia Wesleyan College (where he earned that institution's first ever degree in English with a concentration in creative writing) and his teachers and fellow students at the Muse Writers' Center in Norfolk, VA., Kindra McDonald Greene, a great friend who has helped him work on his poems for long years, the kids in his Sunday school class, the Poetry Society of Virginia, and all the poets who have awed and inspired him.

Bill Ayres is working in his seventh bookstore. He teaches a Sunday school class for five year old children at Wycliffe Presbyterian Church. He has had poems published in *Commonweal, The Anglican Theological Review, the Windhover*.... Why does he look like the dangerous character in the "Sonny" poem? Is it because of the J-shaped scar on his nose?

www.ingramcontent.com/pod-product-compliance
Lightning Source LLC
Chambersburg PA
CBHW021153090426
42740CB00008B/1075